Let's PLAY!

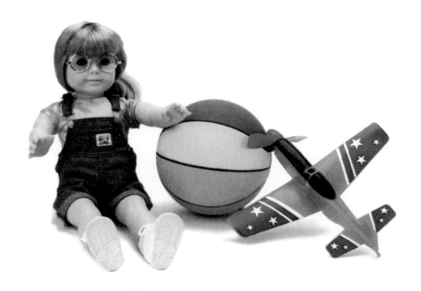

Written by **Lynn Bryan**   Photographs by **Michael Provost**

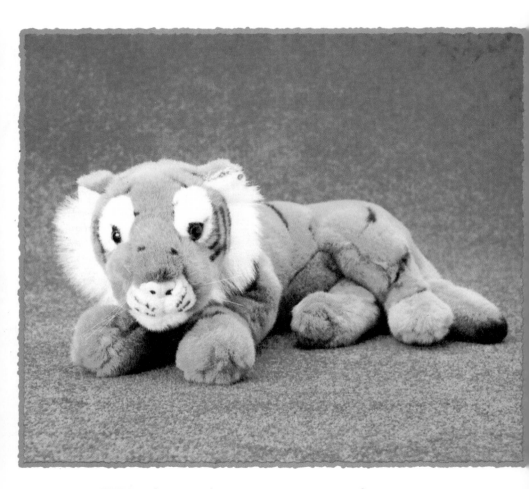

This is my tiger.

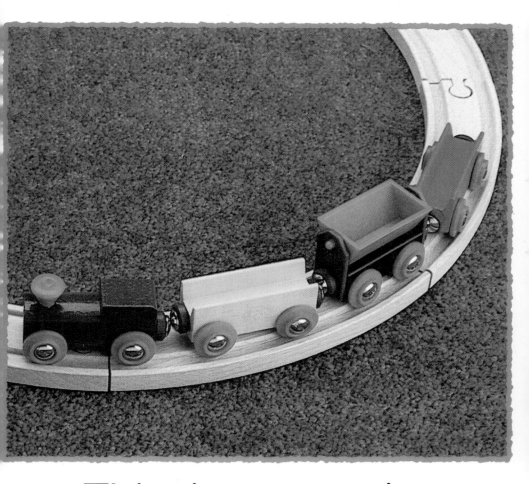

This is my train.

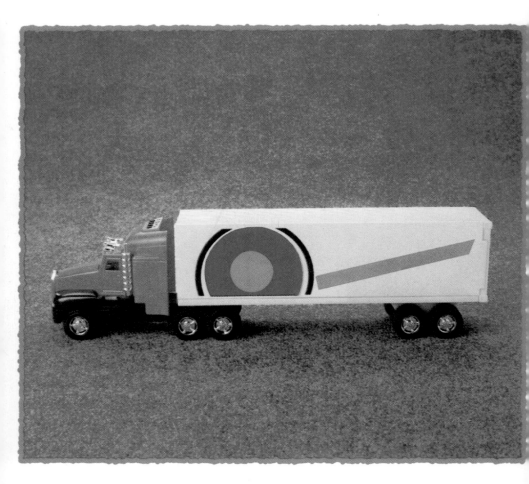

This is my truck.

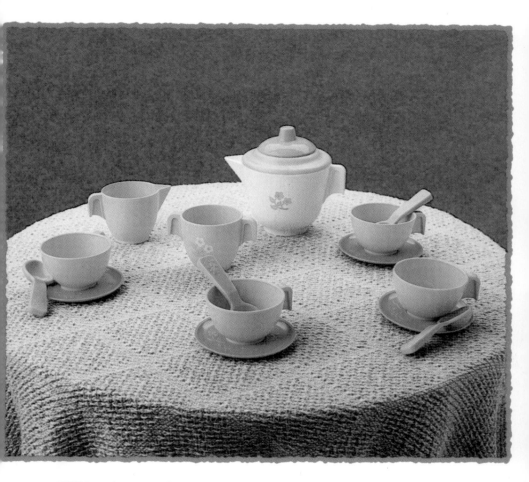

This is my tea set.

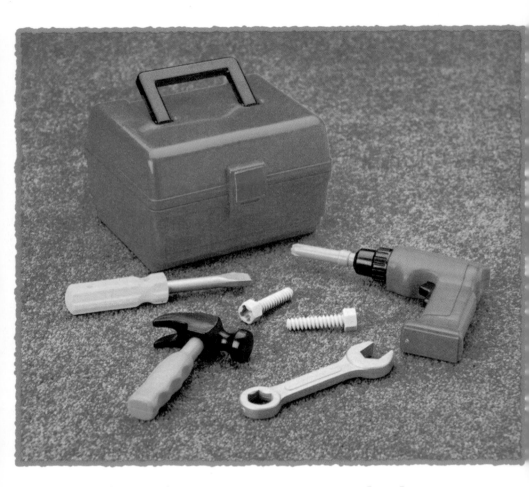

This is my tool box.

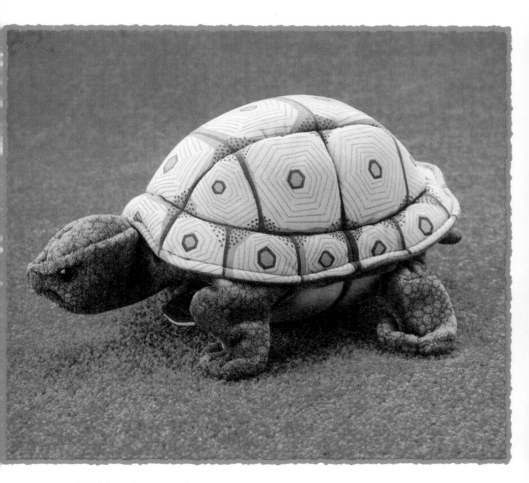

This is my turtle.

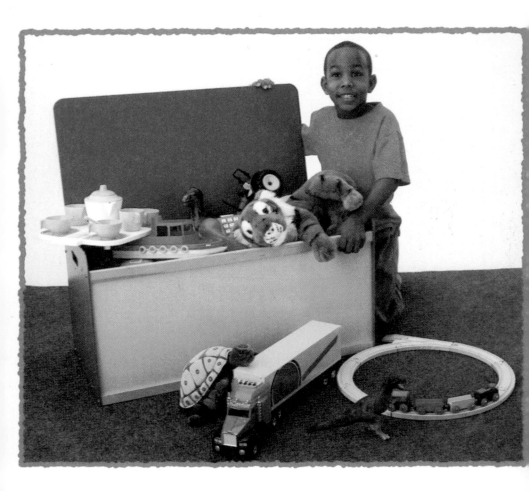

Let's play!